Indian Mythology

R RADHAKRISHNAN

Published by Radhakrishnan R, 2022.

INDIAN MYTHOLOGY

First edition. May 7, 2022.

Copyright © 2022 R RADHAKRISHNAN.

ISBN: 979-8215028346

Written by R RADHAKRISHNAN.

To Ganesha

and to my father R.Ramamurthy for the gift of reading.

Introduction

The Rishis, the wise men of ancient India, were in a dilemma. They had compiled the Vedas, the rules of behaviour, and Dharma had been conceptualised or framed.

Dharma, you could consider as a mission statement for life.

But how to reach it to the people so they could understand? How to ensure that people listened to the lessons? One of those wise men then came up with the brilliant idea of telling stories which would interest people and also have the required knowledge to learn from.

So were born the marvellous stories or epics of Hinduism. The stories have in them ideals, morals, rules of life and so much more. It brilliantly packaged these ideals in stories that enchant and yet teach.

The two great epics of India, the Ramayana and the Mahabharata, are called ithihasa, which roughly means "this is how it happened".

Many Hindus consider these as history and not stories or mythology.

The Epics, especially the Mahabharata, tell us not only stories, they describe the geography of the land, how people lived, it discusses dharma and rules of living; it tells you the history of its characters and how life was then.

It also discusses philosophy and has one of the greatest books written in the world, The Gita.

It also has advice on administration, ruling the land and how to live, which is relevant today as well.

So, storytellers came to a village or a city, and people sat around a campfire and listened as these storytellers captivated them with these tales.

Later, in folk forms like Yakshagana, Kathakali, traditional plays, these stories became dramas, and the storytellers became singers, actors and enacted the stories under flickering lamps.

The stage would be open fields where cultivation was over and the next season was yet to come where travelling troupes would enact these stories. Dance drama forms like Kathakali were enacted inside the temple premises.

For Kathakali, there would be a platform much lower than the stages you see now. The light would be from oil lamps. There would be no backdrops or any special effects. The singers and the instrument players would be at the side or back of this stage. You sat cross-legged on the soft sand of the temple. The height of the Kathakali "thatt", the stage, was ideal when you sat like this.

The performance would start in the night after dinner. Throughout the day, the drummer would drum up a rhythm called the keli kottu, announcing the play that they would stage that night.

The performance would go on through the night and you would sit mesmerised as the singer sang the story and the dancers in traditional colourful Kathakali costumes brought the story to life with their dance. It was the old story teller sitting and telling stories around a campfire.

Now you have performances that are on a modern stage, back drops, sound systems, plush seating, air conditioning and all modern conveniences. But the charm of those old days when those colourful characters came on to the stage in flickering lamplight was much more.

These stories, in one form or the other, are there in almost all parts of India. There are regional variations and there are folk traditions. Some changes are minor and some are major. But they all have one thing in common: they enchant and they educate.

So, gather around the campfire as I tell you some of these stories which you may not find in mainstream versions.

The Song and the Story

Folk tales and folk songs have a different perspective from regular mainstream versions.

If women sing the folk songs, the perspective will be different.

If women alone sing the folk song, the perspective will be even more different.

In a patriarchal society, the voice of women gets suppressed but in folktales and songs, these get expressed.

We see that in the lovely story of Draupadi being protected by the women, which is retold later in this book.

This is a retelling of a folktale from Karnataka on the perils of not listening to a woman or stifling her voice. Which is very relevant even today.

Gangamma lived in a remote village in the Kingdom of Mysore. She was a lively bubbly child who loved to hear stories and sing songs.

When she came of age, her parents got her married to Somanna, who lived in a village nearby.

Somanna was a serious man, elder to Gangamma. He frowned upon songs and stories as frivolous pursuits and spent his days in rituals, study, and working his land.

Gangamma became like him, her songs and stories forgotten, a sad, lonely woman.

But one story and song still lived within her. As time went by, they became stifled inside her and got angrier and angrier.

Finally, they could bear it no longer, and the song and the story decided to take revenge on this couple who had imprisoned them.

One day when Somanna was out in the fields, a tired Gangamma lay down to rest. She fell asleep with her mouth open. The song and the story escaped through her open mouth.

As they wanted revenge on the couple, the song became a shirt and hung on a peg. The story changed to shoes and went and positioned itself near the doorway.

Somanna, when he came in the evening found the shoes at the door and inside he found the shirt.

A suspicious Somanna asked Gangamma, "who has come to our house, who do they belong to, this shirt and shoes."

Gangamma did not know and could not answer and Somanna fought with her. The couple argued back and forth, each sure of their own truth.

Now that's what happens in many marriages, each partner believes in his or her truth alone. This leads to a loss of trust, the foundation of a marriage.

An angry Somanna refused food and in a huff went to the village temple to sleep. That's what men do to make a woman feel guilty. An unhappy and angry Gangamma let him go.

Now those were the days when each house was lit by oil lamps. At night when the lamps were put off, the flame of the lamps all go and reside in the temple for the night.

The flames all meet and sing songs, tell stories, and relate what happened in their houses and have a good time.

That night the flame from Somanna and Gangamma's house reached late and looked tired.

The other flames gathered around and asked this flame why it was late.

"Oh, the silly couple fought for no reason. The woman had a song and story inside her. The couple would not let them out. They escaped and to take revenge they changed to a shirt and a shoe. The man suspected the woman, and they fought late into the night." Said the flame.

Somanna, lying in the shadows of the temple, heard this and wanted to run and tell Gangamma this. But the flames were there, and he had to wait till the morning.

At first light, he ran home and told Gangamma the entire story, but she remembered no song or story now. The shirt and shoes had also vanished.

Since then, women sing and tell stories and men have to listen, that is the secret of a good marriage.

The Mahabharata a quick glimpse.

This book contains some little-known stories from the Mahabharata. This is a small gist of this great epic which is the biggest epic in the world. It will help you understand the context of some stories in this book.

It is said what is not there in the Mahabharata is not there in any other book.

The Mahabharata is one of the two great epics of India. Almost everyone in India knows the gist of the story. This great epic has touched every corner of our country, India.

The original version is the Mahabharata by the sage Vyasa, who himself plays a significant part in the story.

Other than the above version there are so many other versions too. In many parts of India, there are local traditions and stories which are at variance with what is there in the key version.

These local stories add to the charm of this universal tale of two feuding families.

The kingdom of the Kurus is a vast empire which had many illustrious kings. The story narrates the events that led to the great war at Kurukshetra.

There is Bhishma, the crown prince who takes a vow of celibacy and gives up the throne so that his father King Shantanu can marry Satyavati.

Bhishma is the ideal man to rule the kingdom, well trained in the arts of war, Dharma and administration of a kingdom and yet he gives up his responsibility to the country and its people to fulfil his father's desire and lust.

Dhritarashtra and Pandu are brothers, the sons of Bhishma's step brothers, grandsons of Queen Mother Satyavati.

Dhritarashtra is the eldest, but blind, and thus Pandu is crowned the king, which is always a sore point with Dhritarashtra.

Pandu gets cursed that if he enters conjugal relations, has sex, he will die and so he goes to the forest with his two wives, Kunti the elder wife and Madri his second wife.

They crowned Dhritarashtra king, or rather regent, till a proper heir was born, either to him or Pandu.

Dhritarashtra and his wife beget hundred sons and one daughter. Duryodhana is their eldest child and Dushasna the second son. These 100 sons were the Kauravas.

Meanwhile, in the forest with the help of a mantra Kunti has three sons, Yudhishthira the eldest who is Dharma incarnate, Bhima the strong, and Arjuna the Archer. Madri also has two sons with this mantra, the twins Nakul and Sahadeva. The five sons are called Pandavas, after their father, Pandu.

Because of the curse he has received, Pandu dies when he tries to have sex with Madri, he is cremated in the forest and Madri joins him in the funeral pyre out of guilt.

Kunti comes back to the capital Hastinapur with the five children, who are accepted as the sons of Pandu and brought up as princes befitting their status. The great Guru Dronacharya trains them in the arts of war, ethics, Dharma and about ruling an empire along with their cousins, the Kauravas.

Yudhishtra is the eldest of both the Pandavas and the Kauravas. He is also the best suited for ruling because of his calm nature and adherence to Dharma.

They crown Yudhishtra the Crown Prince much to the dismay of Duryodhana and Dhritarashtra.

Duryodhana then plots to kill the Pandavas, along with his scheming uncle Shakuni.

In this story of a family struggle for power, step in many characters.

Karna is the abandoned illegitimate child of Kunti born before her marriage.

By the rules of the day, he is also a son of Pandu. He is elder to both Yudhishtra and Duryodhana and has all the qualities to be a great king. But the abandoned child has been brought up by a chariot driver and his wife, so they consider Karna a low born person.

No one knows he is the son of Kunti, abandoned when he was born. Karna does not know who his actual parents are. He is much better than all the others as a warrior but they do not give him his due and taunt him as being a low born.

Only Duryodhana accepts him and treats him with honour, and becomes his friend. The Pandavas take every opportunity to belittle and humiliate him, leading to an enmity between Karna and the Pandavas.

Kunti, though she knows Karna is her son, never divulges the secret while he is alive.

On the eve of the great battle, Kunti reveals the secret of his birth to Karna, and then asks him to join the Pandavas. She tries to tempt him with the Kingdom. As the eldest of all, he would be the ruler of the Kingdom.

But Karna remains steadfast in his friendship but promises his mother that he would not kill four of his brothers, he will kill Arjuna or get killed by Arjuna. Thus Kunti will still be the mother of five sons.

Karna is a generous, large-hearted man, and he makes Kunti promise not to reveal the secret of his birth as long as he is alive, as that would make the Pandavas hesitate in the battle.

He knows this will lead to certain death for him but he accepts that and thus Karna goes to his death for the sake of friendship.

Karna is the tragic hero of the Mahabharata, whom everyone who reads the Mahabharata loves.

Krishna is in a way the main protagonist of the story, an avatar of Vishnu he is born to establish Dharma. He supports the Pandavas and is the guiding force behind their victories.

When all seems lost, Krishna steps in and saves the day. The Pandavas are just instruments, Krishna is the actual doer in the story.

Krishna is one of the most popular gods in India even today. He is charming, wily, and ruthless when required. He is focused on the goal and in the Bhagavad Gita he expounds on life and its meaning.

The Mahabharata is full of twists and turns and finally reaches a climax in the eighteen-day war in which most of the warriors meet their end.

The Pandavas finally have their victory but it is hollow as they have lost all their kith and kin, including their children.

Hanuman and Garuda: Pride and Fall.

Hanuman and Garuda are both great devotees of Vishnu, the god who protects the world. But the lord sometimes feels he has to teach his devotees a lesson.

Hanuman is one of the most popular gods. He is unmatched in strength, intellect, and all the qualities.

Hanuman is self-effacing and totally devoted to Rama.

Hanuman is exemplary, but Garuda gets carried away and this is a tale of how the Lord brought him back to reality.

Garuda, the king of birds, is the vehicle of choice for Vishnu. Garuda carried him everywhere and everyone associated Garuda with Vishnu.

Garuda was ever alert, strong, tireless, a protector of devotees and dharma. He was an imposing and imperious presence, which brought a sense of awe in all who met him.

All this, and to be ever with Vishnu, gave Garuda an aura.

Vishnu was the preserver of the world. To be associated with the lord gave Garuda a high. He showed off and looked down on others. He considered himself the foremost bhakta or follower of Vishnu and expected others to recognise this and defer to him.

Vishnu had taken avatar as Krishna and was bothered by all the preening by Garuda.

Hanuman, that great devotee of Rama, lived unobtrusively in the Himalayas. Rama was also an avatar of Vishnu, born to rid the world of Ravana.

The age of Rama was long over. This was the Dwapara yuga when Vishnu had come in his Krishna Avatara.

Hanuman was one of the immortals, revered the world over for his strength, his knowledge, and above all for his steadfast loyalty to Sri Ram.

Hanuman was never one to show off. He remained in the background and only when required would he come forth. In Krishna's time, he lived a quiet life in the far mountains. He rarely came into the world of men.

As Garuda's ego swelled, Krishna decided it was time to teach him a lesson.

He sent a message to Hanuman to come to Dwarka, enter the royal gardens, and eat all the fruits there. If anyone disturbed him, he was asked to lay waste to the garden.

Hanuman, with no hesitation, reached the royal gardens of Dwarka.

It was the season for mangoes. The royal garden was full of different varieties of mangoes. From the large banganapalli, the sweet Kesar, the shapely totapuri, all varieties of mangoes were spreading their heavenly aroma.

The gardeners went in the morning to the garden and found a large scruffy monkey there happily eating the juicy mangoes.

It was, of course, Hanuman. He followed the lord's instructions faithfully. But as usual, he came as a normal nondescript monkey and not in his normal appearance.

The gardeners tried to shoo him off, but he bared his large yellow teeth and chattered at them. The gardeners were timid and did not want to get bitten by a scruffy, rabid monkey. He also looked quite dirty, so they did not want to touch him.

They tried to drive him off by throwing stones and sticks at him. But the monkey was agile. It caught whatever was thrown at him and flung it back with an unerring aim.

The gardeners were at their wit's end. They asked the guards for help. The guards stood there laughing, but at this they became silent.

There were very strict instructions from Balarama, the elder brother of Krishna. No harm was to come to any living thing within the palace. Balarama was a strong and fierce warrior and apt to be short-tempered, but he was also a very kind man. The soldiers did not want to get into his bad books. They could not shoot or spear the monkey because of this order from Balarama.

So, they tried to trick or cajole the monkey out of the garden. They brought delicious sweets and snacks from the royal kitchen and kept them outside the garden to entice the pesky monkey.

But the Lord had said to eat the fruits in the garden, so the monkey ignored all the delicious stuff from the kitchen and continued feasting on the fruits.

The gardeners and the guards watched as the monkey ate all the mangoes. They could not believe a monkey could eat so much.

The guards waved their spears and tried to frighten the monkey. The monkey got annoyed at their attempts and snatched a spear, chased, and spanked a few of the guards.

The dejected soldiers and gardeners then approached Krishna, who always gave a sympathetic hearing to his people.

Krishna listened to them, smiling inwardly. Garuda stood near, looking mockingly down his beaked nose at them. He was sure these people were exaggerating.

Krishna glanced at Garuda and asked him, " What do you think I should do, old friend? Shall I go myself or put up the matter to Balarama".

Garuda laughed, " This is such a minor matter, leave it to me" and strode out to get the pesky monkey and bring him to Krishna.

"Don't hurt him, he is just a monkey, and be careful," said Krishna as Garuda was going out. Garuda waved dismissively. A monkey, Krishna thought he should be careful of a monkey. He smiled to himself.

The monkey was contemplating an overripe jackfruit, that strong-smelling fruit of the tropics, when Garuda strode into the Garden.

Without saying a word, Garuda caught hold of the monkey by his neck to march him to Krishna.

The monkey scowled and chattered at Garuda, snarling in anger and showing large yellow teeth.

Garuda said, " Behave yourself now, I am just taking you to my Lord Krishna. If you don't behave, I will have to take harsh measures against you."

The monkey stopped its struggles and snarls. It smiled and easily twisted out of Garuda's grasp. The monkey then smashed the overripe jackfruit over Garuda's head.

With the powerful smell of the ripe fruit in his nostrils and fruit dripping all over his head and body, Garuda lost his temper.

The watching guards and gardeners were now laughing at Garuda. The monkey stood there chittering and smiling at him.

This was the last straw for Garuda. He forgot Krishna had told him to be careful and not hurt the monkey.

With a roar that filled all those who heard it with fear, Garuda rose into the air. His eyes wild and red with anger, Garuda flashed down with unmatched speed. He was going to buffet the monkey senseless with his powerful wings. He was going to rake him a bit with his sharp talons.

He hit the monkey hard, but surprise, surprise, the monkey did not move or even seem to feel the blow.

The monkey seemed to look mockingly at Garuda. An infuriated Garuda called on all his strength and slashed at the monkey with his talons.

The monkey moved aside and looked at Garuda with contempt. The monkey's long tail curved and before he could react Garuda was caught in its coils.

Garuda was surprised and ashamed. A common monkey was not only able to withstand his blows but also trap him in its tail!

Roaring with rage, Garuda tried to break free. The people watched as the mighty Garuda strained and struggled in the grip of the monkey's tail.

All the while the monkey went on eating the fruits calmly without even bothering to look at Garuda.

A tired Garuda finally stopped struggling and politely requested the Monkey to release him. He also told the monkey that Lord Krishna had ordered him to be brought before him.

At last, the monkey turned towards him, Garuda noticed then that he had calm and wise eyes

The monkey let him go but shrugged his shoulders at the orders from Krishna, and with one bound vanished.

An astounded and dejected Garuda came before Krishna and reported all that had happened.

Krishna smiled at him and said, " That was no ordinary monkey, that was my dear devotee Hanuman".

Garuda was annoyed he felt they had tricked him. And Hanuman had refused to obey Krishna!

Krishna sighed; Garuda still had not learnt his lesson. He told Garuda;

"Hanuman is fully focused on me, in my Rama avatar. He will listen only to Rama. For him everything else is transient. Go to the Himalayas and request him politely to come here. Tell him Rama wants to see him."

Garuda flew to the Himalayas and found Hanuman in his normal form. He was no longer a scruffy monkey.

Simply dressed, his muscular arms and chest bare in the snow-clad mountains, Hanuman was meditating when Garuda appeared.

With no animosity, Hanuman, with humility, welcomed Garuda and offered him a seat next to him.

But Garuda was uncomfortable. He did not want to prolong this. He stiffly accepted Hanuman's greetings and conveyed to him that Rama wanted him at Dwarka.

Without hesitation Hanuman stood up and said, " Brother Garuda, we will meet at the palace gate."

Garuda nodded and smirked. He was the king of birds. He could fly faster and higher than anyone. Garuda took off on a soaring flight. He would reach first and show Hanuman who he was.

Meanwhile, in Dwarka Krishna with his Maya, the power of illusion changed Shesha, the king of snakes, to look like Lakshmana. Lakshmana was Rama's brother, and both he and Hanuman were fond of each other.

Krishna then changed his wife, Satyabhama, to look like Rama's wife, Sita.

Satyabhama was rich and proud of her wealth. She was happy that she could tease a lowly monkey.

Krishna then called his Sudarshana Chakra, the celestial weapon which could not be withstood by the most powerful beings in the universe. He programmed the Sudarshana to guard the palace doors. No one was to be allowed inside, irrespective of who he was.

Meanwhile, Garuda landed before the palace gleefully expecting to show off his speed to Hanuman.

But there was a stalwart figure standing patiently in front of the doors. Hanuman had already reached and was waiting for Garuda.

An abashed Garuda moved forward, saying:

" Come Hanuman, I will take you to the lord."

But the Sudarshana chakra blocked the way. It resisted all efforts by Garuda to enter. Garuda was getting embarrassed. He was using all his powers but could not overcome the chakra.

Hanuman watched this impatiently. He was eager to meet Sriram and had enough of this farce. He reached out and caught the Sudarshana chakra, put it in his mouth and kept it there like he would have any morsel of food which he planned to eat later!

Garuda, stunned, looked with his mouth open at Hanuman. "Come, Sriram is waiting," said Hanuman, and went inside.

Krishna was waiting there, and as soon as Hanuman saw him, he rushed forward eagerly, his face transfused with joy. Krishna lifted him and embraced him.

Shesha, in the guise of Laxmana, greeted Hanuman. Hanuman looked at him surprised and asked him, "why are you dressed as Laxmana, Shesha"?

He then turned to Krishna, who brought forward Satyabhama, who was disguised as Sita. " Here is Sita waiting to meet you Hanuman, seek her blessings"

Hanuman turned towards Satyabhama and smiled " I don't know who this proud lady is, Lord, she is not mother Sita. But I will seek her blessings as ordered by you, Lord." and Hanuman prepared to prostrate before Satyabhama.

Krishna stopped him, laughing at an amazed Garuda. "Where is my Sudarshana, Hanuman"? Krishna asked.

Hanuman looked apologetic. " I am sorry, my lord, but in my eagerness to see you, I put it in my mouth, as it was annoying me. Here it is." He said in all humility.

Garuda was abashed. Hanuman was so focused on the Lord that to him, nothing else was important. Even Krishna's Maya, which beguiled everyone, did not affect Hanuman.

The Sudarshan Chakra, the most powerful weapon, was but a toy that could not impede a devotee like Hanuman from seeing the Lord.

Garuda had learned his lesson.

A temple for Duryodhana

Duryodhana strides the Mahabharata like a raging colossus. A villain who has a public image of being a black and jealous villain who coveted his brother's property.

This image is a later creation of popular pulp fiction, movies and TV serials

In the Mahabharata of Vyasa, he is a well-etched character with a lot of good in him and justification for his stand.

In every person there is both good and bad. Whether we are good or bad depends on us and how we control the evil in us. Duryodhana was a good prince, but his envy of the Pandavas led him into actions that were bad.

Alas, the victors write history and mostly Duryodhana was portrayed as a bad person.

Duryodhana lies helpless and dying after being unfairly attacked by Bhima.

Bhima, in a harrowing and horrible act, kicks Duryodhana in the face.

An angry Krishna stops Bhima from doing anything further to the fallen prince.

Duryodhana tells Krishna, mocking the Pandavas, " I have lived a good life, have studied the Vedas, made gifts to many, I have ruled this world and stamped out my enemies. I have had a happy life and now I am on the way to heaven, having died a warrior's death. I am luckier than the Pandavas who will have to continue living in this world of sorrow having lost so many who are dear to them."

Duryodhana smiled and continued, "I also do not mind Bhima stamping on my head. After a while the crows and vultures will peck at my head and eyes."

Hearing this, flowers shower on Duryodhana from the heavens.

The Pandavas hang their heads in shame.

Duryodhana, till the end, did not repent any of his actions and believed he was in the right.

What he said as he lay dying was true in many respects. He was a kind king and unlike the others, looked at people on their merits and not on their caste or birth.

His acceptance and friendship with Karna are proof of his egalitarian view.

A story from Kerala highlights this attitude of his.

The Pandavas were in exile, and during the last year had to remain incognito. If the Kauravas found them, the Pandavas would again have to go into exile.

Duryodhana was searching for the Pandavas so that they could again send the Pandavas into exile. He searched the whole of Bharat varsha as this land was then called and had reached Kerala.

It was a hot and humid day and Duryodhana, true to his impatient nature and incredible strength, was very much ahead of his men.

It was a forest interspersed with small fields with a hillock. A thirsty Duryodhana searched for water and saw a small house nearby.

He walked into the house and found an old lady inside. On his asking for water, she offered him toddy, a fermented drink given to honoured guests.

She could see from his dress and ornaments that this was a great high-born king. She doubted whether he would accept anything from her hands, as she was a Kurava, a local tribal from whom people of the higher caste would accept nothing, especially food and water.

Duryodhana was different and would not do any such unfair discrimination. He happily accepted the drink from her, enjoyed it, and thanked her.

He then climbed the hillock and prayed to Lord Shiva for the prosperity of the local people, who were also his subjects, his praja, as he considered them.

He then gave acres of land to the Kuravas and the other local people there for their life and sustenance. Thus, these landless tribal communities became landowners because of Duryodhana.

No ruler, till then, had bothered about the welfare of these poor people. Such was Duryodhana, impatient and short-tempered, but also a kind man who did not worry too much about social restrictions.

Today in Malanad, in the Kollam district of Kerala, is a temple to this prince on the same hillock where he prayed.

The temple has no idol or deity installed. Instead, it has a platform where you can sit and pray to God as you imagine or wish.

Duryodhana is considered the Sankalpa Murthy at this temple. Sankalpam is the process by which you focus your intent when you pray.

To this day, the taxes for this temple are paid in the name of Duryodhana as the owner of the land. The priests are all from the Kurava Caste.

An abiding memory of a kind prince by his people, who were neglected by others.

Presumption and Perception among Friends

Friendship, especially childhood friendships, can suffer because of presumption and perception.

All of us have all experienced it.

We are friends in school; we drift apart and meet again after years. In our eyes, we are the same, and we believe the other person is also the same.

Years later, we meet with great joy and open our hearts.

We look at each other through the prism of time. What we see is a distorted image.

Life and our experiences have changed both of us. We don't realize this and sometimes the friendship gets a jolt, and it hurts both.

In this situation, one of us, at least, has to turn the page and move forward in the book of life.

If we do not, we will only continue the hurt and belittle ourselves and the friendship we had.

Drona, before he became an acharya, was close friends with Dhrupad, the prince of Panchala. They were both students at the ashram of rishi Bharadwaj, who was the father of Drona.

At the ashram, the others looked up to Drona. He was a brilliant student and the son of the guru. Dhrupad was a prince, but not a talented student.

Drona would often help Dhrupad in his studies, and the grateful prince would promise to share everything, including his kingdom, with his friend Drona.

They completed their ashram studies and went their separate ways. Drona became Dronacharya, a master and teacher of the art of war and all weapons.

Dhrupad, in due course, became the king of Panchala.

Drona was a poor brahmin. He and his family survived on whatever alms he received. Drona, as a teacher, did not have many students. He could not establish an ashram of his own. But he was content and did not strive to get a better position.

But then he had a son, Ashwatthama, and for his sake, Drona wanted to earn some material benefits.

He remembered his friend Dhrupad. He was sure that Dhrupad remembered him.

He presumed Dhrupad was still that old friend of his who looked up and deferred to him.

Dhrupad had become a powerful king. He was feared and respected everywhere. He was a good man at heart, but power has its effect on the ego.

Drona strode into Dhrupad's court. He saw his old friend sitting on the massive throne. He was happy he presumed it was the old duffer prince, who always deferred to Drona, who was sitting on the throne.

Dhrupad saw a poor brahmin before him. The powerful king presumed that this was another person who wanted to trade on old relationships. Dhrupad did not perceive a friend; he saw a beggar.

It upset Drona when he received such a cold welcome. His ego was bruised. Here was the duffer in pomp and glory while Drona, the brilliant student, struggled.

Drona perceived an ungrateful friend, and not the king on the throne.

Instead of sweet words of friendship, he harshly recalled Dhrupad's promise to share his kingdom.

Dhrupad rose in a rage. He saw a beggar who instead of supplication was demanding, and that too half his kingdom!

Drona had no intention of asking for half the kingdom; all he wanted was a cow, but at the insult, he perceived from one whom he presumed to be a friend lesser in knowledge. Anger took hold, and he demanded half the kingdom.

Dhrupad, equally angry, replied to this demand by saying harshly " You are a beggar, I am a king. Once we were friends when we were children who did not know better. Friendship is between equals, not between beggars like you and a king like me. I will give you cows, gold and land and not punish you as you are a brahmin."

A raging Dronacharya, in open court, made a promise. He shouted "Dhrupad, you fickle and false friend, keep your cows, gold, and land. I Drona promise you; my students will defeat you and I will meet you as an equal".

Fortune's change, Dronacharya became the guru of the Kuru princes. As Guru Dakshina, the fees a student offers to his guru on completion of studies, the Pandavas defeat king Dhrupad, take him captive and offer his kingdom to Dronacharya.

Dronacharya keeps half the kingdom and returns the other half to Dhrupad.

"Dhrupad, we are now equal and can be friends," says Dronacharya.

Dhrupad pretends to accept and Dronacharya presuming all is the same as before goes back crowning his son Ashwatthama, the king of half the kingdom.

An angry Dhrupad wants revenge. He does a yagna, which is an offering to the gods, and gets a son, Dhristdyumna, who is destined to kill Drona. He is the twin brother of Draupadi, who becomes the wife of the Pandavas.

Dronacharya teaches Dhristdyumna the art of war even though he knows Dhristdyumna is destined to kill him.

During the Mahabharata war, Dhristdyumna was the commander-in-chief of the Pandava army.

He leads the Pandavas to victory, though at great personal cost. He loses his father and his three sons who are killed by Dronacharya and Karna.

In anger, Dhristdyumna killed Drona while Drona had relinquished his weapons and was sitting in meditation.

The war is over on the 18th day; the Pandavas relax. Dhristdyumna is finally sleeping. Ashwatthama, the son of Dronacharya, sneaks inside the Pandava camp with a few followers.

He catches Dhristdyumna unarmed, and they beat him. Dhristdyumna begs for a sword so that he can die an honourable death.

Ashwatthama, his father's death fresh in his mind, refuses, and Dhristdyumna is beaten and smothered to death and then beheaded. An ignoble death for a warrior.

Ashwatthama pays for this and other crimes by losing his Nagmani and cursed to wander forever unwanted everywhere, seeking a death that never comes. If he does not die, he cannot attain moksha, salvation.

Thus, two friends turn enemies and start a circle of violence that brings nothing but hurt, hate, despair and death.

Anger, ego, and violence solve no problems, they only start a chain of unhappiness. The wise person moves away from any action based on anger, ego, or violence, as they only lead to disturbance and misery.

In the next story, we will explore another story where two friends both understand each other so well that their friendship continues even after life changes for them.

Friendship Sudama and Krishna

Friendship is a mix, complicated, simple, sublime, misery, and happiness. Our stories are full of friends and their relationships.

Our ancient epics and puranas explore the various facets of friendship.

There is the friendship between Karna and Duryodhana. A friendship that redeems them. Karna willingly gives up everything and lays down his life for Duryodhana.

If Karna had accepted Kunti or Krishna's offer, Karna, as the undisputed elder of both the Pandavas and Kauravas, would have become the emperor. But he felt it would be a betrayal of his friend and so he goes to his death keeping his royal birth a secret.

There is the friendship between Draupadi and Krishna. One where Draupadi can talk freely about her problems and even scold Krishna.

There is friendship and betrayal between Dronacharya and Dhrupad. Which leads to violence, war, and misery.

So many stories exploring the different facets of friendship.

But for pure friendship, nothing comes close to that between Krishna and Sudama or Kujhelan as they called him in south India.

In the ashram of guru Sandipani near Ujjain, Sudama and Krishna were students.

Sudama was a poor brahmin boy, the son of Matuka and Rochanna from Porbandar in Gujarat.

Krishna was of Royal Yadava lineage and the socio-economic difference between them was vast.

In the ashram or gurukul, all students are equal and do all the required work together.

One day Krishna and Sudama were deep inside the forest collecting firewood.

It started raining, and both took shelter under a tree. As time went by, Krishna felt hungry and asked Sudama if he had anything to eat.

Now Sudama had some plain beaten rice, poha, with him, but it was old, parched, and had little taste. For a poor boy like him, it was enough, but for Krishna, a royal Yadava, it would be poor fare.

So Sudama kept quiet, the rain still came down and Krishna again asked, "Friend Sudama, I am hungry have you got nothing for me."

Sudama hesitantly opened the small bundle of poha and offered it.

Sudama watched in wonder as Krishna ate this poor fare with great relish. Krishna did not laugh at him or his poverty. Krishna smiled at him sweetly, hugged him, and thanked him.

From that day onwards, the two became close friends. They were different in all respects, but still became close friends.

The well-off Yadava royal who charmed everyone, mischievous, outgoing, and confident. The poor brahmin boy, shy, hesitant, an introvert.

They grew up learning together and devoted to each other.

The day came when they completed their studies and had to part. They promised to keep in touch, but years and distance took their toll.

Sudama practiced his vocation of teaching and worship. A simple man, he did not prosper and was content with his life.

Krishna became famous, a warrior, an adviser to kings he was the most famous person around in a few years.

Krishna and his Yadavas came and settled in Dwarka, which is near Porbandar where Sudama lived.

Sudama in due course married Sushila, a lady from a family as poor as him.

They had children and things were difficult for the poor family. Even one meal a day was proving difficult.

Sushila nagged Sudama to approach Krishna, who was part of the ruling family in the land, for help.

But Sudama cherished his friendship and was afraid of asking Krishna for help. He felt it would demean and affect their relationship. He felt it would be wrong on his part to presume upon the friendship and ask Krishna for anything.

Now, this differs from Dronacharya's behaviour where he presumes on his old friend and demands half the kingdom from Dhrupad!

But Krishna is after all Krishna, and he understands Sudama's plight. One day Sudama hears a voice from outside his poor hut.

"Oh, Sudama, I am hungry and am waiting for you," says a very familiar and beloved voice.

Sudama rushes out and there standing outside his hovel is Krishna, richly attired and dazzling, with that captivating mischievous smile and his twinkling eyes.

Sudama, deeply moved, rushes forward to meet his dear friend. Sudama, ashamed of his poverty, does not invite Krishna inside his house.

They both sit outside, talking about old friends and happenings. Krishna smiles and tells Sudama, "Dear friend, I am hungry will you not feed me?"

Sudama has nothing in the house but some beaten rice saved by his wife which was to be their meal for that day.

Sudama goes inside and his wife gives him the beaten rice. Krishna happily accepts and eats it with relish.

Sudama is happy to meet his friend and offer him what he could. He never speaks of his needs; his joy is in just meeting his friend.

But when Sudama turns back after seeing off Krishna he finds his hovel has changed into a grand house full of all that he needs and his wife and children well dressed.

Krishna understood his friend's needs without Sudama asking for it.

But Sudama is not happy as he worries, he has lost his friend's regard and goes to visit Krishna.

Sudama walks to Dwarka from Porbandar, carrying a pouch of beaten rice, lovingly made by his wife as a gift.

Dwarka is the first city of the land, and Krishna lives in the biggest and most opulent palace in this grand city.

Sudama hesitates at the entrance in awe at the surrounding magnificence.

There are fierce Yadava warriors at the gate who look at the frail and ordinary Brahmin with curiosity.

As Sudama hesitates to enter, Krishna, who knows everything, comes to the gate himself.

He lovingly embraces his friend and gives him a royal welcome. The people of Dwarka wonder who is this nondescript man given so much importance.

His friend's affection touches Sudama, his doubts assuaged. He does not voice his doubts but Krishna understands and his actions comfort Sudama, who cries in happiness.

The friends sit happily sharing the beaten rice brought by Sudama. Krishna's wives and the others look on in wonder as Krishna forsakes all the delicious food of the palace to eat plain beaten rice with his friend.

Sudama is happy, and returns home and leads an austere life, happy that his friendship is intact. He now has sufficient wealth now to take care of his family. He remains a simple man, devoid of any pretension, even though the lord himself is his friend.

Krishna smiles at his wives and explains, " Sudama is devoted to me, my friend seeks my friendship first, for Sudama that is most important, I respond to that love and affection he has for me."

Karna and Earth's curse

Governance is all about connecting to people and having empathy with them.

Today, when even petty Government officials show no empathy and throw their weight around, this is a story from ancient India which highlights the empathy of a ruler.

A retelling of the story still relevant today.

They had crowned Karna, King of Anga, and unlike other kings, he was an affable and accessible ruler.

His adopted parents, who were common people and not of the royalty, had brought Karna up.

Karna thus knew first-hand the troubles of the common people and was always there for them. He was also a kind and generous man and would help anyone who asked for his help.

In his capital, he would walk among the people and not ride in a chariot or on a horse. The people became accustomed to seeing their king amidst them, like anyone else.

One day Karna was walking on the street alongside the market when he came upon a small girl holding a small oil can and crying on the side of the road.

He noticed that the earth had oil on it beside the girl. He understood that the girl's oil had spilled.

True to his nature, he stopped, sat beside her, and tried to comfort her. He promised to buy her some more oil.

But that did not console the girl. She wanted the same oil that was spilled on the ground.

A child is adamant when an idea takes hold and we adults normally ignore their wishes. We don't consider the child's view or happiness.

But Karna was Karna, large-hearted, putting others' happiness before his happiness and always facing his troubles with courage.

His empathy was also with the girl, as someone who had very little while growing up. He knew how even a little wastage hurt.

He smiled affectionately at her and asked her to hold up her vessel. He took the oily mud and squeezed the earth between his powerful palms.

The people watched in wonder. Karna was an incredible warrior, one of the greatest of his time. He was the King too. But there he sat on the ground with oily mud between his palms beside an ordinary little girl.

A man of incredible strength honed over the years by using the bow; the earth was squeezed dry between Karna's hands.

The people watched in awe as drop by drop the oil was squeezed out and into the vessel held by the little girl.

At last, all the oil was recovered and the little girl smiled her thanks and went off blithely, not knowing it was her King who helped her.

The people also left, and Karna dropped the dried earth from his hands. As he was getting up, he heard a groan of pain. He stopped and looked around, but found no one. But still he heard the groans and wails of pain.

The sounds seemed to come from the earth he had squeezed. Karna picked up the earth and found mother Earth's face crying in the lump of dry mud.

Karna was shocked. He held the earth tenderly and begged her to stop crying and tell him why she was crying.

Mother Earth glared at him and said, " Oh Karna, you are a powerful warrior. You should not have used your strength to squeeze me so much. I am hurt and in pain. Your action is not the action of a warrior."

Karna bowed to her in salutation and replied, "Mother, that child was crying and needed my help. If I am at fault, I am sorry but I need to help when anyone needs my help. Especially when they are the citizens of my kingdom. I am deeply saddened to have hurt you and will accept whatever you deem as my punishment. "

Mother Earth was angry. She was angry that Karna, while acknowledging his fault, did not seem to have regrets.

" Karna, you have hurt me, and I cannot forget or forgive that. One day I will catch you and hold you like you have held me today. That day will teach you how it is to be helpless in someone's grip." Said Mother Earth in anger.

Karna bowed his head at this and said, " I happily accept this, mother, for the pain I have caused you. "

Karna went back to his palace and we know that, later, at that crucial moment when Karna was battling Arjuna, the wheel of Karna's chariot caught in the mud and all his efforts to get it free were unsuccessful. It was at this moment, when Karna was not armed and busy trying to get the wheel free, Arjuna killed Karna.

Arjuna did not kill Karna. Karna's deeds, both good and bad, killed Karna.

This story also tells you the need to take care of the earth or suffer the consequences. An environmental message from an epic written so long ago.

The man with two wives

We find many people today who take both sides depending on how the wind blows. Such people are called opportunists, but they call themselves practical.

But what happens when we try to ride two horses at once, well it is like marrying two women at the same time. It lands you in trouble.

This is a story of one such man in ancient India.

In a city in the south of India lived a trader named Sukeshan, a very rich man who traded all over the world.

When he was young and just starting his business, his parents got him married to a young woman who was chaste, hardworking, and came from a good family.

He was a handsome man with long silky locks of hair, hence his name Sukeshan, the one with beautiful locks of hair.

As the years went by, his business grew and so did the affection between him and his wife Parnika.

The family grew because of this affection. Parnika gave her lord two children who were the apple and mango of her eyes.

A boy with silken hair like the father with nothing else, and a girl as intelligent as the father. But the children are irrelevant to this story so we will leave them be.

Now it so happened that Sukeshan, like all men, had a roving eye and one day that eye fell on the young and energetic dancer Ojasvani.

One thing led to another and our hero soon danced to the tunes of the young dancer.

The young lady too got attracted to Sukeshan and soon both were the talk of the town.

Sukeshan was much older than Ojasvani but that did not deter the lovers, who one day got married in front of the magistrate of the town.

The news of this reached his petite wife, the calm and patient Parnika.

Now Parnika means little leaf, and the lady was like a little leaf, small and delicate.

But Parnika is also another name for Parvathi, the Goddess of strength who lives in all wives. When she manifests herself in the wife, all husbands quake and shiver in fear.

When Sukeshan returned home the next day with his young new bride, it was this manifestation of the Goddess that he saw.

Parnika was furious, and Sukeshan could do nothing but wring his hands, shiver and nod.

Ojasvini would have none of this. Those days a man could marry more than one wife if he was brave or foolish enough.

Ojasvini was energetic, and she could battle with the best. Sukeshan found himself between the devil and the deep sea.

But Sukeshan was also a leading citizen, and the clamour reached the mayor of the town.

The mayor called the three of them and got an agreement made between the three of them. They would have to abide by it or face the consequences.

The two ladies would have separate houses and Sukeshan would spend alternate days with each.

The plan seemed to work, and all was well for a few years.

As age caught up with him, Sukeshan began to get grey hairs.

Those days there were no hair dyes and Sukeshan could not do much to hide them.

When Ojasvini saw the grey hairs, it upset her. People would think she married an old man. So, she carefully plucked all the grey hairs from Sukeshan's head.

The next day Sukeshan, with his glossy black locks of hair, went home to his elder wife Parnika.

Parnika had aged gracefully along with him and she, naturally, had grey hairs.

Parnika massaged a tired Sukeshan's head with coconut oil as was their routine when she saw he had no grey hairs.

Parnika was upset. If people saw her husband had no grey hair, they would think he was younger than her.

Now that would never do.

Society looked at older women having younger husbands with suspicion.

We have evolved little as a society, and today also look at a woman with a younger husband with suspicion.

So Parnika plucked out all the black hairs. Poor Sukeshan, when Parnika finished, his head looked like a marble. It was all shiny with the oil and no hair was to be seen.

So Sukeshan, named for his beautiful hair, lost his hair and his identity.

Now that happens if you try to please everyone, the ultimate loss will be yours.

Mandodari Ravana's wife.

The Indian view is starkly different from the western view as regards good and evil.

Life is not black and white, Dharma itself is not a fixed constant, it may change with the person and situation.

Unlike other religions, Hinduism does not have one book which alone constrains its adherent's behaviour. There is no single dogma or theory or practice which alone defines the religion.

The belief in Hinduism is that we are all part of universal consciousness and that this consciousness also exists in all of us.

This leads to the premise that in everyone there is good and there is also evil. When the evil in us is dominant, we behave badly.

But there is also good in everyone and so the evil characters of our epics and stories have redemptive qualities too.

The characters are never fully evil or fully good, at times they go with the flow, and are supported by truly good people too.

Mandodari, the wife of Ravana, is one such good person who is steadfast in her love for Ravana.

We have made Ravana into a larger-than-life villain today, but he had many excellent qualities.

Mandodari is one of the "Panchkanyas" five exemplary women whose name itself is enough to dispel Sin! And this lady is Ravana's wife!

She is a woman lost in the epic because of the larger-than-life husband she has.

There are various stories from different sources as to her birth. In many stories she was created from a frog, Manduka in Sanskrit, hence called Mandodari.

There are many interesting stories about her birth, especially in the Andhra and Odia folklore. But most of them are not in sync with the character of Mandodari as described in the Ramayana.

So, for our story, we will go with the one from the Ramayana.

In the Ramayana, she is the daughter of Mayasura, the king of demons, and his apsara wife Hema.

Mayasura visits swarga, the abode of the Gods and there he marries the apsara Hema and they have three children, two sons Mayavi and Dhundubhi and a daughter Mandodari.

There is a small town in Madhya Pradesh, Mandsaur, the headquarters of the district of Mandsaur. The residents claim that Mandodari's maternal home was Mandsaur and so Ravana is their son-in-law. To this day, in some parts of the town, they do not burn Ravana's effigy on Dussehra.

Mandodari is a beautiful woman, chaste and devoted to Ravana. She is proud of his strength, his kindness to his people, his knowledge but is also aware of his fatal flaw, a weakness for women.

She loves him with non-judgmental love, accepting his faults, including his lusty nature, leading him into trouble and finally, this weakness leads to his death.

Mandodari considers herself superior to Sita by birth and beauty. Ravana, Mandodari's husband, is besotted with Sita, but even then Mandodari tries to protect Sita from Ravana. She repeatedly urges him to restore Sita to Ram.

Sita devoted to Ram and does not give in to Ravana's desire. Ravana could not force himself on Sita because of a curse he had received.

Frustrated, Ravana decides to kill Sita rather than allow her to go back. He draws his sword to behead her, but Mandodari, who is there, grabs his hand, preventing him from doing so. Ravana is a great warrior and when he is in a rage, no one dare go against him. But Mandodari dares, and to Ravana's credit he loves and respects Mandodari and so listens to her.

She convinces Ravana that killing Sita would be a blemish on his reputation as a great warrior. She pleads with him to send Sita back to Ram and avoid the war.

But Ravana, blinded by his ego and lust, does not listen to Mandodari's wise counsel. He spares Sita but will not return her back.

He goes to his doom and death at the hands of Rama.

Mandodari, distressed, desolate, devastated and disarrayed, comes to the battlefield where Ravana lies dead.

Mandodari has lost her sons, her relatives, and her husband, the great Ravana, who was the greatest warrior and king of his times.

Mandodari weeps and laments for her dead husband and lover. But her grief is also tinged with the knowledge that this resulted from Ravana's own actions.

Unlike the ladies in the Mahabharata or other puranic stories, Mandodari does not lose her balance, she does not blame anyone or curse Ram or the others in anger.

In Valmiki's Ramayana, Mandodari fades away after Ravana is killed. There is nothing more about this remarkable lady.

But there are other stories of how she agrees to marry Vibhishana, Ravana's younger brother, so that Lanka is saved.

The people of Lanka would not accept Vibhishana as the successor of Ravana, their beloved king. Vibhishana defected to Rama, deserting his brothers and family just before the war. The citizens of Lanka don't like him; the situation is delicate and fraught.

A civil war could break out.

Mandodari is preparing to join Ravana on the funeral pyre, as she has no interest in life now after having lost her beloved husband and her sons.

Rama stops her and convinces her that for the good of her kingdom and people, she should live and marry Vibhishana.

By marrying Mandodari, Vibhishana would gain legitimacy and be accepted by the people of Lanka. This would avoid a disastrous civil war in Lanka.

For the sake of her people, Mandodari agrees and marries Vibhishana and also helps him govern the land and heal the wounds left by the war.

There are many other stories of Mandodari, all of which show a woman of great knowledge, balanced, true to her principles, and always rooted in both dharma and reality.

A truly remarkable woman.

Draupadi's protectors.

The Ramayana and the Mahabharata are pan-Indian tales. The cast of characters is huge and the stories themselves have local variations.

There are of course the mainstream versions which have minor changes and the changes are nuanced to reflect local ethos and empathies.

There are also folk traditions that are very different in some respects.

This is such a folk story from Tamil Nadu.

A version not from books but an oral retelling that has survived over the ages.

It is a touching tale of empathy very relevant even today.

In the traditional version of the Mahabharata, during the game of dice, Yudhishtra loses his brothers and his wife Draupadi, gambling them away as wagers.

The Kauravas drag Draupadi to the court where the game of dice is being played.

Duryodhana orders her to be disrobed in front of everyone.

As no one comes to her rescue, Draupadi prays to Krishna, who protects her by miraculously ensuring that her saree is never-ending and Dushasna finally gives up.

In the Tamil oral version, this story is different. This is a retelling, my version of what I heard long, long ago in a small village near Pondicherry.

Yudhishtra is in the clutches of gambling fever and, like all gamblers, has a brain fade.

Yudhishtra, the intelligent embodiment of Dharma, has lost his wits and all his possessions to the Kauravas.

As Shakuni keeps rolling the dice on the Kaurava side, the other Pandavas watch aghast as Yudhishtra wagers them, his brothers, and loses them.

Bhima, Arjuna, Nakula, and Sahadeva have to remove their royal jewels and dresses and wear the clothes of servants.

Yudhishtra, still in the clutches of his passion for gambling, then wagers himself and loses.

Yudhishtra stands dressed in servitude, having lost his kingdom, his possessions, his brothers, and finally himself.

Yet the passion for gambling is still strong in Yudhishtra and the taunts of the Kauravas egg him on.

Draupadi, that peerless princess, married to all the five Pandava brothers, is a desirable woman.

Draupadi is beautiful, intelligent, passionate, and fiery.

Duryodhana hates her with a passion for real and imagined slights, even though she is his sister-in-law.

Urged by the Kauravas, Yudhishtra wagers Draupadi in one last throw of the dice.

Draupadi is in the women's quarters, along with the other ladies.

Being among the family members, Draupadi dressed casually. She was having her menses, her periods, so she wears only a wrap-around lower garment, a ravikkai, a bodice, to cover her breasts and an utariya, a traditional piece of cloth or garment used to cover the upper part of the body.

The ladies were chatting together, discussing marriages, relationships, quarrels, and everyday life. Unlike the men who postured and strutted about with fragile egos, the women got along well together, making adjustments so that life went on smoothly.

They feared this talk of war and anger. In the end, it was the women who would lose whoever won.

The messenger from the court came in at that moment and the message was " Duryodhana had summoned Draupadi".

The message was strange. Why would Duryodhana summon Draupadi?

The messenger was reluctant to explain but under the questioning of the senior ladies; he narrated the happenings in the court.

A horrified Draupadi is stunned and in shock. The other ladies, too, are in shock.

If Yudhishtra, the man reputed to be Dharma incarnate, could behave so badly under the influence of a passion for gambling, they shuddered to think what lesser men would do.

Draupadi rose in anger and shouted at the messenger, " Ask the emperor Yudhishtra, did he lose himself first or me. If had already lost himself he has no right to pledge me as a wager".

The other ladies, both royal and the serving maids, murmured in agreement.

The messenger went to the court and hesitantly repeated Draupadi's question.

Duryodhana flared up at this and asked the soldiers there to drag Draupadi to the court.

There was an animal growl from Bhima which terrified the soldiers, who were hesitant to enter the women's chambers.

Reluctantly, the soldiers approached the women's chambers and stopped at the entrance. No man but one from the family could enter, said the ladies.

The soldiers hurried back and reported to Duryodhana.

Duryodhana roared in anger and frustration, but he knew once the women took a stand, he could not do much.

The women included his mother, wife, sister, aunts and so many others he could not look in the eye and command.

His brother Dushasna, a stalwart man, stepped forward. He was blindly loyal to his elder brother, Duryodhana. For Dushasna, everything began and ended with his brother.

Dushasna was not an evil man, he was just a man.

He said, "Brother let me go and I will drag her here by her hair".

The court was full of grand men. Men of honour, men of valour, men reputed for their generosity, men of wisdom. Great men all, they kept silent.

Dushasna strode into the women's quarters. He brooked no interference.

Draupadi saw him, and so did the other ladies there. He strode forward and caught Draupadi by her hair.

There was silence as the women were in shock. Then Draupadi rose in anger " How dare you Dushasna? I am your bhabhi, elder brother's wife. How can you lay hands on me? Have you no shame".

Dushasna shrugged and replied, " It is Duryodhana's wish, and you are now a slave belonging to us. You have no rights. Your husband has wagered and lost you".

Struggling in his grip, the frail Draupadi looked helpless. But her spirit was strong, eyes flashing as she railed against Dushasna. " Yudhishtra cannot wager me after losing himself. Let go of me, you shameless man."

But Dushasna was remorseless as he dragged the princess, the honour of his family, through the corridors and steps of the palace.

The women followed, aghast and horrified. Royal ladies, serving maids, cooks, laundresses. The group of ladies grew as Dushasna dragged a wailing and screaming Draupadi through the palace. Though she was hurt in mind and body by the violence and the indignity she suffered, Draupadi still fought every inch of the way.

Finally, Dushasna dragged her into the court where he stood, wiping his brow and posturing as if he had won a grand victory.

A sobbing Draupadi looked around. Her five husbands stood there, the Pandavas, noble warriors who could defeat anyone, including the Gods.

Arjuna, her favourite among the Pandavas, the archer without equal turned his face away, tears in his eyes.

Passionate Bhima, the strongest man in the world, looked at his feet, his face suffused with anger and shame.

Nakul and Sahadeva stood with downcast eyes. Draupadi turned to Yudhishtra, her husband, eldest of the Pandavas, acclaimed as the epitome of Dharma, the righteous man.

She felt the anger rising anew, along with bile, as she looked into his sanctimonious face. Yudhishtra gazed back at her, devoid of expression.

Draupadi asked Yudhishtra, " you had already lost yourself after that you cannot wager me, how did you do that".

The learned Yudhishtra replied, " Even if I had lost myself, you were still my wife and I may wager you".

Draupadi looked away in anger and frustration. The women who had gathered in their strength looked at Yudhishtra with disdain. They looked at the mighty Pandavas and the anger in their eyes scorched the Pandavas.

Draupadi looked at Bhishma, the grand old man, the patriarch of the family. He was a man of firm principles, but he looked away, not able to meet her eyes.

The women gathered there also watched along with Draupadi, who now looked beseechingly at Dronacharya, the Guru of the Kauravas and Pandavas. One word from him would stop this, but he remained silent, his eyes fixed at some distant view.

Dhritarashtra was blind, and he would remain dumb, too, today. Karna was a generous, honourable man. Draupadi looked at Karna and saw only an angry man enjoying her distress. Karna was not generous enough to forgive or forget the words she had addressed to him during her swyamvar.

Draupadi and the women looked at all the men in that court but none stepped forward.

At last, there was a man who stepped forward. Yuyutsu, the half-brother of the Kauravas, stepped forward. Yuyutsu was the low born son of Dhritarashtra, and a serving maid. He folded his hands and addressed

Dhritarashtra " Oh King, my father, stop this inhumane behaviour or our family will lose its good name".

Vikarna, another of the Kaurava brothers too, stepped forward, adding his voice to Yuyutsu.

But the blind king was also dumb and deaf on that day. Their brothers, the Kauravas, shouted down Yuyutsu and Vikarna and pushed them out of the court.

Draupadi and the women watched the drama unfolding before them with despair.

"Remove her clothes, Dushasna," ordered Duryodhana, baring his thigh, "We will make her sit here".

Dushasna strode forward and laid his hand on Draupadi's utariya, the top cloth that she wore.

Draupadi clutched at it, wailing for help, but the men stood around without coming to her help.

A few looked ashamed, some indifferent, and many looked on with interest.

The women were now wailing along with Draupadi; her being disrespected, tortured, and shamed, touched a chord in them.

The women felt her pain, her despair, her frustration. It was their pain, too.

As Dushasna finally ripped off the utariya, there was a rustle among the women and a young, lowly maid came, removed and dropped her utariya on Draupadi covering her. The girl herself was exposed, but she stood there protective over Draupadi, the disgraced queen. A lowly maid who dared to oppose the world of men.

Dushasna shoved the maid away and pulled at this new covering on Draupadi. Another of the maids ran forward, removed and dropped her utariya on Draupadi.

Draupadi looked, wondering at these two low maids, and folded her hands to them.

Dushasna growled and caught hold of this utariya too, but as soon as he removed it, there was another in its place.

The women crowded around, the royal ladies, the common maids, the cooks, the washerwomen, all of them. There were no distinctions now. They were all together, women in a man's world. The mothers of the men were there, the sisters, the wives, the mistresses, the concubines, the dancing girls all together as they bared their chest and dropped their utariyas on Draupadi.

Dushasna was tired; he had dragged a struggling Draupadi all over the palace. He removed one piece of cloth and there was immediately another in its place. The ladies jostled him, and he fell.

Draupadi sat there, tears of gratitude dropping from her eyes, her hands folded, acknowledging the shared empathy with the women.

Duryodhana looked at the women and saw the determination there.

Karna saw the women as more generous than he could ever be.

The Gurus dropped their heads; they had been taught a lesson today.

The women lifted Draupadi and carried her away as the men looked on, silent and in shame.

Iruvan the Perfect Prince.

The Mahabharata, they say, contains everything that you can think of and to a large extent that is true. It is at its core a story of human beings, their strengths, weaknesses, greed, ego, lust, relationships and how it affects their life.

There have been many stories added to the major story over a period. Many stories do not find themselves in the main story, as they are not considered pertinent or are uncomfortable.

The story of Iruvan is one such tale.

Arjuna the Pandava broke the agreement between the five brothers regarding their common wife, Panchali. As per the agreement, he had to go into exile for 12 years.

Arjuna wandered over the land during these twelve years and had many adventures. Arjuna, being Arjuna, also has many dalliances. He reached the northeast of the country and there he fell in love with Uloopi, the Naga princess.

They marry against the wishes of Uloopi's brother and have a son called Iruvan. Arjuna, as all men do, talks of his responsibilities and greater tasks awaiting him and leaves both the wife and his son and continues with his travels. Uloopi too does not wish to leave her land and her people to go amidst strangers in a far-off land.

Iruvan grows up into a dazzling boy, the apple of his mother's eye. Hated by his maternal uncle but protected by his mother, Iruvan grows up to be a formidable warrior. He keeps hearing the stories of his famous father and dreams of becoming like him and meeting him one day.

Grown to adulthood, he goes to Indraloka, the abode of the Gods to meet his paternal grandfather Indra.

At Indraloka he meets his father Arjuna, and both of them are emotional at the meeting and Arjuna can barely hide his pride on seeing how stalwart a warrior his son has grown up into.

The Kurukshetra war is imminent, and Arjuna seeks the help of his son for the war. Iruvan happily promises to come whenever Arjuna wants.

Uloopi is not happy at this turn of events, but Iruvan is adamant and she relents finally as Iruvan is a warrior and she hopes they will accept him in the Kuru family.

Iruvan arrives at the battlefront and is warmly welcomed by the Pandavas and the family. He fights on the side of the Pandavas and proves to be a heroic and formidable warrior.

With his skills with weapons, his army of serpents, the nagas, his mastery of maya, the art of illusion; he proves to be a thorn in the side of the Kauravas. Warriors famous for their prowess are no match for this valiant prince.

A desperate Duryodhana, the Kaurava prince, leader of the opposing army, then asks the Rakshasa Alambusha to kill Iruvan.

Both the warriors are evenly matched. Alumbusha is a master of maya, the art of illusion. He assumes the form of Garuda; the enemy and destroyer of serpents and kills the protecting serpent army of Iruvan.

Iruvan breaks Alambusha's bow and cuts him to pieces, but Alambusha's body reforms. Such is the power of the Rakshasa. Iruvan keeps cutting him up but Alumbusha reforms. At last, a tired Iruvan who has been fighting many warriors since dawn is beheaded by Alumbusha. Thus dies the brave and valiant son of Arjuna.

Now the above is what appears in most of the mainstream Mahabharata stories.

But in the south, especially in the land of the Tamils, there is a disturbing darker story, one that touches upon so many emotions and can sear the soul.

There are many variations, but in all the stories the young prince pays a terrible price.

The Pandava gather before the great battle, as do the Kauravas, to discuss strategies and action plans.

Duryodhana, the Kaurava prince, approaches Sahadeva, the Pandava prince who is the foremost astrologer of those times.

Bound by his duty, Dharma, as an astrologer, Sahadeva, has no choice but to advise Duryodhana, his enemy.

He advises that the day after tomorrow on Amavasya or new moon day would be the ideal time to make a human sacrifice to the battlefield.

This was a practice where a warrior who was most suitable sacrificed himself for the victory. Amavasya was also the day when one did tarpanam, offerings to one's ancestors.

There are four perfect men suitable for the sacrifice, Krishna himself, Arjuna the Pandava, Shalya King of Madra and maternal uncle to the Pandavas and the young perfect prince Iruvan.

King Shalya had a large army and had been tricked by Duryodhana into fighting for him against the Pandavas.

Krishna was Krishna and on the Pandava side. Arjuna was the chief warrior on whom the Pandavas depended. Arjuna was also the sworn enemy of Duryodhana and the Kauravas.

This left the young and naïve prince Iruvan. Duryodhana was the elder cousin of Arjuna, and thus an uncle to Iruvan. He meets Iruvan and convinces him to sacrifice himself for the Kauravas on the day after tomorrow.

Pleased with himself, Duryodhana leaves the Pandava camp, but unknown to him Krishna is watching and realizes the plan.

He discusses this with the Pandavas and advises them that the only way to avoid a catastrophe is to have Iruvan sacrifice himself for the Pandavas.

Poor Iruvan is again put under pressure and the Pandavas with Krishna's help convince Iruvan that it is his prime duty to sacrifice himself in the war for the benefit of the family.

The young prince succumbs to the pressure but advises that he has already given his promise to Duryodhana to offer himself as a sacrifice the day after tomorrow. Krishna smiles and promises to take care of that issue.

Iruvan then seeks two boons for the sacrifice.

First, that he should be married and enjoy conjugal bliss.

The second boon he seeks is that he should be able to watch the entire battle. Krishna again smiles and agrees to the boons.

The Pandavas and everyone are puzzled how Krishna will manage all this. Krishna tells the Pandavas to arrange for the sacrifice the next day and also to arrange for the marriage of Iruvan immediately, as there is only one night left now before the sacrifice.

Sahadeva is puzzled and worried. The auspicious time for the sacrifice would be on Amavasya night when the new moon forms. Amavasya was two nights away and here was Krishna proposing that the sacrifice be done one night earlier! But his faith and belief in Krishna keeps Sahadeva quiet.

The Pandavas dress Iruvan in all his finery, and the perfect prince is the cynosure of all eyes. But no woman comes forward to marry him. No father will give his daughter to one who will die on the morrow.

The Pandavas offer immense wealth and even offer half their Kingdom if they win the war. But all this avails them nothing, and time is running out. As is their wont, in times of trouble they run to Krishna and seek his help.

Krishna sighs, but he cannot disappoint his devotees and agrees to help. The Pandavas are happy and go off to see to the arrangements for the marriage.

Krishna, with his maya, transforms himself into Mohini the celestial damsel without peer. The most beautiful woman in the world.

Mohini approaches the wedding mandap and agrees to marry Iruvan. Everyone is dazzled by this beautiful couple, and the wedding is celebrated with gaiety and happiness. The time now comes for the couple to enter their room and enjoy their one night of conjugal bliss.

The young couple consummate their marriage, Iruvan tells Mohini that he asked for marriage so that he could be cremated and receive all the funerary offerings which would ensure that he does not linger in this world.

Also, he has now become aware that his father and his family are only interested in him as a vessel for victory and their mourning would contain an element of joy as they would now hope that their victory is certain.

Iruvan wants to be mourned wholeheartedly, and he believes his wife would do so.

He is desolate that his father and uncles who should have protected him wish to offer him as a sacrifice for their own ends, whether it is the Pandavas or the Kauravas.

Krishna resumes his normal form and goes for his ritual bath in the river and thereafter his bath offers tarpanam, the ritual offering to one's ancestors, which is done on Amavasya or new moon day.

The others, especially the Brahmins and Sages, watch Krishna and are surprised, as per their calculations Amavasya is the next day. But they all know that Krishna is Narayana, the protector, and believe he can do no wrong. Their calculations must be in error, they think and emulate Krishna and offer tarpanam to their ancestors.

Surya and Chandra, the sun god and the moon god, watch this from above and are disturbed. They decide to confront Krishna together and get him to stop.

They appear before him and with folded hands request Krishna to stop, as the Amavasya is only on the next day.

Krishna welcomes them and in return asks them what Amavasya is all about. They both reply that Amavasya is the occasion when both of them appear together and there is no Earth between them.

Krishna then points to them and they realise they are together, and there is no Earth between them. Krishna has ensured that Amavasya has occurred a day earlier.

The worried Surya and Chandra then return to Indraloka and seek Indra, King of the Deva's help. How the problem of Amavasya coming one day earlier is resolved is another story, and we will revert to Iruvan.

It is new moon night that day and after dusk a sombre group of people in the Pandava camp meet in the hall of sacrifice on the Kurukshetra battlefield where the Kali, the Goddess of the battlefield is invoked to accept the sacrifice and ensure the victory of the Pandavas.

Iruvan, dressed in all his finery, approaches at the appointed hour. The prince willingly makes the initial offering of his flesh on behalf of the Pandavas. What they leave can be used by Duryodhana and the Kauravas, as the promise to them is for the next night.

Iruvan removes his epaulets, his breastplate and all his armour. He takes the sanctified knife and cuts his body into thirty-two parts, one part for each perfection as a perfect man is believed to have 32 perfect qualities.

These thirty-two parts of Iruvan's body are then picked up one by one by Yudhishtra, the eldest of the Pandavas and offered to Kali while the perfect prince lies dismembered and suffering on the floor of the chamber. The Pandavas and their supporters are happy now that the sacrifice has been done and their victory assured.

The sacrifice is over and Iruvan lies on the floor of the chamber, bleeding to death, all alone in his agony.

Mohini, Iruvan's wife, comes and takes his head on her lap and wails and cries out for her loss and Iruvan dies in her lap.

The Pandavas then cut his head and put it up on a pole high up, and the head watches the entire battle from there.

In Tamil Nadu there are thirty temples to Iruvan or Koothandvar, as he is called here. The most prominent temple is in the village of Koovagam.

Here at the Koovagam temple, during the months of April and May, there is an annual festival which is attended by transgenders from all over. The transgenders, and even some men who have taken a vow, marry Iruvan, and they spend the night in happiness and joy of a marriage.

But the dawn brings death and desolation, and the bereft wives of Iruvan mourn and wail their loss as once Mohini did.

Their families have abandoned the transgenders; sacrificed for their social status, they are dead for their families.

Iruvan is dead, but he lives on in the memory of his followers as the perfect prince sacrificed by his family for their victory.

This is a retelling of the folktale, and there are many other variations of the above tale. We can explore them some other day.

Notes and suggested readings.

Indian Mythology is a vast treasure house of stories. One of the biggest sources are the two epics.

The Mahabharata and the Ramayana are known all over India and a basic knowledge of the story is known to all Indians irrespective of the religion they follow.

For those who has not read the Mahabharata or the Ramayana the following books are suggested as initial reading. They are mainstream versions and may not contain the stories that I have retold here.

1. Amar Chitra Katha Comics have a large collection of stories from Indian Mythology. They also have comics with an abridged version of both epics.
2. The Ramayana by C. Rajagopalachari published by Bharatiya Vidya Bhavan remains a classic. It is written in simple language and is a concise version of the Epic.
3. The Ramayana by Kamala Subramaniam also published by Bharatiya Vidya Bhavan is a more detailed version but still only abridged version of the original epic.
4. The Mahabharata by C. Rajagopalachari published by Bharatiya Vidya Bhavan remains a classic. It is written in simple language and is a concise version of the Epic and yet captures its essence.
5. The Mahabharata by Kamala Subramaniam also published by Bharatiya Vidya Bhavan is a more detailed version in a single volume.
6. For those interested in exploring folklore the works of A.K Ramanujan will be of interest.

There are many other versions and modern writers have explored the epics giving their own view point and creating fresh stories.

I have read and heard many versions of the stories in the Ramayana and the Mahabharata.

During my travels and posting in different parts of India I found that each area had local stories and songs about the characters in the two Epics.

This sparked of my lifelong love and search for stories based in the epics but with a local twist.

The stories included in this volume are only a few of those stories being told and retold by the people of India over the centuries.

I hope you enjoy reading them.

I would love to hear from you at my email id krishnanrr2622@gmail.com.

My Facebook page is R.Radhakrishnan

| Page

Did you love *Indian Mythology*? Then you should read *Rustic Romeo*[1] by Radhakrishnan R!

Travellers Tales

Rustic Romeo

R.RADHAKRISHNAN

2

A tangled triangle of tea and love!

In rural India of the late eighties two brothers well past thier prime battle for the love of thier life.

A humorous and whimiscal short tale from India.

Filled with all the colors, chaos and vibrant life of interior India, Radhkrishnan transports you into another world full of humour and rustic charm.

Read more at https://sites.google.com/view/rradhakrishnan.

---

1. https://books2read.com/u/mKyOg9

2. https://books2read.com/u/mKyOg9

Also by R RADHAKRISHNAN

The Temples of India
The Temples of India: Somnathapura, Mysore

Travellers Tales
Rustic Romeo

Standalone
The Colors of Life
The Temples of India : Guruvayur
Indian Mythology
The Book of Ancient Wisdom

Watch for more at https://sites.google.com/view/rradhakrishnan.

About the Author

Radhakrishnan retired from Indian Oil Corporation Limited after a career spanning three decades and postings in many parts of India.

He is a traveller who enjoys the journey more than the destination.

An observer, never intruding or judgemental, he writes with humour as he watches the whimisicality and eccentricity of life in all its glorious colors.

He now lives in the picturesque city of Cochin in Kerala with his wife and two kids.

Read more at https://wordpress.com/home/ thepassageofmind.wordpress.com.